Original title:
Crickets and Couplets

Copyright © 2025 Creative Arts Management OÜ
All rights reserved.

Author: Maya Livingston
ISBN HARDBACK: 978-1-80567-186-2
ISBN PAPERBACK: 978-1-80567-485-6

Two Voices, One Melody

In the night, two friends sing,
A duet of silly things.
One hops high, the other low,
Creating a comical show.

They chirp of cheese and flying pies,
About the best way to disguise.
Joking loudly, then they pause,
What's that noise? A round of applause!

The Chirping Chorus

A band of bugs in perfect sync,
With melodies that make you think.
They crack up with a silly rhyme,
Joking about the passing time.

One forgets the notes to play,
Just starts dancing halfway.
The laughter echoes in the air,
As others join without a care!

Rhythms of Dusk

As sunset paints the skies so bright,
The critters gather for delight.
They trade their tales in quick exchange,
With punchlines that are often strange.

One criticizes a bad tune,
While others laugh and whistle soon.
The rhythms clash—a funny mess,
A night of laughter, no less!

Secrets in the Silence

When quiet falls, the whispers grow,
As secrets pass from toe to toe.
What funny tales do they concoct,
In the stillness where they are locked?

One speaks of hats that float away,
While others giggle, trying to stay.
In silence rests a hidden jest,
With laughter lingering, never at rest!

Vows Under the Moon's Gaze

Two lovers sat beneath the beams,
Whispering sweet romantic dreams.
But then a cricket stole the show,
With chirps that made their laughter flow.

The vows exchanged were quite the scene,
As bugs danced like a ballet dream.
Their giggles rose into the night,
As stars winked at their pure delight.

Threads of Sounds and Silences

In the stillness, a sound arose,
Tickling hearts like ticklish toes.
A chirp, a buzz, then silence pressed,
Their laughter burst; they were so blessed.

A symphony of unexpected glee,
Combined the sound of cricket and pea.
As each note flew through the air,
They joked about their crazy flair.

Night's Embrace of Harmony

Beneath the stars, a serenade,
Love's melody was softly played.
With every chirp, they twirled around,
In rhythm, love was truly found.

But one critter hit a wrong note,
And off-key sang like a old boat.
They laughed and danced, quite out of time,
As echoes rang like silly chimes.

Harmonies in Hidden Places

In corners of the garden neat,
The local bugs began to greet.
With tiny fiddles in their hands,
They played a tune across the lands.

While lovers watched the funny sight,
They joined the bug band with delight.
And every note made love ignite,
As critters led them into night.

Songs of the Silent Woods

In the woods where no one goes,
A tiny band begins to pose.
With legs for bows and wings for strings,
They play a tune that laughter brings.

The trees sway gently, joining in,
Their leaves a clap, a joyful din.
As shadows dance beneath the moon,
The air fills up with merry tune.

Echoes of Insect Harmonies

Beneath a starry, twinkling night,
A chorus rises to delight.
The little critters take their stage,
Each chirp and hum, a new engage.

One sings low, another high,
Together they shoot for the sky.
The moon just chuckles, gives a grin,
Insect music, let the fun begin!

Rhythms of Dusk's Embrace

As dusk paints skies in hues of gold,
Unseen jesters, bold and old.
With every note, the giggles rise,
A symphony with no disguise.

The laughter echoes through the trees,
A raucous choir carried by breeze.
Nature's jest, oh what a game,
In this twilight, they stake their claim.

Melodies of Nature's Choir

Each evening comes with silly sound,
Nature's jesters gather round.
With tiny feet, they tap and glide,
A wacky show they cannot hide.

They harmonize with glee, no doubt,
As playful chirps begin to sprout.
The audience? Just fireflies bright,
Twinkling softly, oh what a sight!

Starlit Stanzas

Under the moon, the critters dance,
In tiny shoes, they take a chance.
With little tunes that squeak and chirp,
They twist and twirl, then trip and slurp.

A grasshopper leads with a jumpy jive,
While ladybugs laugh, feeling alive.
The night sky twinkles, a winking friend,
As the party goes on, it will never end.

Lullabies of the Meadow

The night is full of chirpy cheer,
With fuzzy friends all drawing near.
A cricket quartet starts to croon,
Their silly songs make the stars swoon.

A firefly winks with a flash of light,
Joining the chorus, oh what a sight!
A badger wobbles, just finding his beat,
And giggles erupt from the tall grass seat.

Nocturnal Serenades

In the still of night, a rhythm's born,
With squeaks and beeps, a tune is worn.
A hedgehog's snore, a frog's loud call,
They mingle together, a concert for all.

A mouse finds a mic made of twigs and leaves,
Telling tall tales that no one believes.
Laughter erupts, as the owls refrained,
In the grand hall of nature, much joy is gained.

Cadence of the Quiet Inhabitants

In the hush of dusk, the chatter begins,
Tiny hosts join in, all love to spin.
An ant brings snacks, all crumbly and sweet,
While the whole crew sways to the fun little beat.

A dance-off starts beneath the bright beam,
Everyone laughing, like they're in a dream.
As dawn approaches, they all claim their prize,
With wings and giggles under brightening skies.

Soft Sounds of the Earth

In the garden, they come to play,
A symphony at the end of day.
They chirp and dance in twilight's glow,
While I try to find my way below.

Robins sing and frogs reply,
All around, the night draws nigh.
But here they are, with all their zest,
Pretending they're the very best!

Enchanted Nocturne

Whispers and giggles mingle at night,
With tiny creatures taking flight.
They think they're stars, sparkling bright,
But really just bugs, oh what a sight!

There's one in a tux, real slick and neat,
Waltzing around on his six tiny feet.
While I chuckle, full of delight,
They twirl in moonbeams, what a flight!

Tales Woven in Moonbeams

Once there was a long-legged chap,
Who tripped on air, oh what a tap!
He thought he broke into a dance,
But ended up in a weird romance.

With a ladybug, they shared a tune,
As they twirled 'round beneath the moon.
And in their laughter, the night grew light,
A comic scene, oh what a sight!

The Gentle Arc of Sound

With each little chirp, a story unfolds,
Of brave little tales that never grow old.
Like a sitcom, they hop and skip,
Unafraid of the impending trip.

Then one takes a leap, what a flub,
Tumbling down like a future celeb!
And all their friends burst into chime,
For laughter, dear friend, is truly divine!

A Conversation Among Stars

In the sky, a sparkle plays,
Whispers from cosmic ballet.
"Do you think we're all that bright?"
"Only when it's dark at night!"

"Meteors race, look at them zoom!"
"Way faster than my room's vacuum!"
"Do you ever feel this small?"
"Only when I trip and fall!"

"Could our light travels be a show?"
"Of course, we're stars, don't you know?"
"Let's blind some cows, causing doubt?"
"They'll never know what we're about!"

"Perhaps we ought to dim a bit?"
"Or have a contest? Who can sit?"
"Only winners get the night!"
"Losers get no comet flight!"

The Dance of Earthly Echoes

Down on earth, the sounds collide,
A tune from nowhere, oh what glide!
"Is that a frog or just a croak?"
"Maybe it's a sleepy bloke!"

"Can you hear that raucous cheer?"
"Just the wind, I think, my dear!"
"Is that laughter from a bee?"
"Or just a sneezy gummy tree?"

"My plants are dancing, look at them sway!"
"Must be the music of the day!"
"Should we join in this merry game?"
"I'd rather watch, it's less to tame!"

"Nature's got its own beat and groove!"
"True but I'm not sure I can move!"
"Let's toast to the echoes we hear!"
"As long as they don't bring me near!"

Love Letters in the Night

Beneath the moonlit sky, they write,
With pens that glow and spirits bright.
Each stroke a giggle, each word a cheer,
Love notes wrapped in laughter's sphere.

A paper airplane flies with flair,
Captures the sighs of two in the air.
They giggle as it lands, a little crumpled,
Their hearts in sync, ever so rumpled.

With secret messages, they communicate,
Between the shadows, oh how they skate!
A dash of mischief in every line,
Their banter dances like sweet sunshine.

The night erupts in joyful sound,
As laughter echoes all around.
Each letter tucked in a wishful fold,
A playful tale that never gets old.

Essence of Evening Whispers

As twilight falls, the chatter begins,
In the garden, where giggle wins.
Buzzing tales and nibbled leaves,
Spinning stories 'til the night believes.

With crumpled notepads and goofy grins,
The secret language of whispers spins.
A titter here, a snicker there,
In every whisper, a playful dare.

Under stars that chuckle bright,
They pen their hopes with pure delight.
In the warm embrace of evening's glow,
Funny tales flow like a gentle show.

Each phrase a jest, each pause a jest,
Their hearts entwined, a light-hearted quest.
In the essence of night, they create a scene,
Where laughter reigns, and love's evergreen.

Notes Carried by the Wind

Floating notes on a gentle breeze,
Tickling the leaves with whispered tease.
The grasshopper joins, a dancer's delight,
As laughter ricochets into the night.

They scribble jokes on scraps so small,
With doodles that daintily sprawl.
The wind carries wishes, flapping like wings,
Where the giggling heart merrily sings.

Twilight chuckles as they unfold,
Their playful secrets, almost bold.
In every rustle and gentle shake,
A melody swirls, for fun's own sake.

The world around them is a stage divine,
Each grassy seat a comfy line.
They toss their notes and giggle anew,
With every breeze, adventures ensue.

Serenading the Starlight

They strum the air with notes of cheer,
Under starlit winks, their laughter clear.
With silly rhymes and joyous tunes,
They serenade the laughing moon.

In the backyard, shadows bloom,
As music dances, dispelling gloom.
With every pick on a twinkling string,
Joyous echoes of love take wing.

The songbirds join in a merriment,
With flutters and chirps, a sweet ascent.
A lilting rhythm, a chuckling spree,
In harmony, they just let it be.

Their melody floats in the crisp night,
A funny tale wrapped in delight.
Under the vast, twinkling cascade,
Their hearts sing loud; they're not afraid.

The Night's Quiet Refrain.

In the dark, a chirp takes flight,
Two insects join, what a silly sight!
They bounce and hop, oh what a show,
A comedy of errors in the moon's soft glow.

Each note a giggle, a silly tune,
They dance together under the moon.
With every chirp, they tease and play,
While sleepy eyes begin to sway.

The leaves all rustle, a risqué cheer,
As they jive and jangle, drawing near.
A couple's quarrel? Oh no, that's dread!
Just two mismatched solos in the night instead.

So if you hear that joyous sound,
Know that laughter's loose and unbound.
And in the night's soft, gentle air,
Two tiny stars are singing there.

Whispers of the Night

In twilight's glow, a whisper springs,
Two voices rise on tiny wings.
With playful tones, they thread the dark,
A duo's jest, a nightly lark.

A chirp for cheese, a chirp for bread,
They bumble forth, a tale to spread.
Their banter rings like silly clowns,
Echoing softly through the towns.

The moonlight laughs, a sly old friend,
As winged companions on wits depend.
They share their dreams of dazzling flight,
In a chorus that lasts all night.

So listen close, don't miss a chance,
Join in the night's absurd dance.
With every chirp, you'll hear delight,
In the whispers of the laugh-filled night.

Harmony in the Grass

In the meadow, a tune takes shape,
With grass as stage, no escape.
Two little stars take center stage,
With banter sparked, they break the cage.

One sings high, the other low,
Together they make quite the show.
A riddle wrapped in a playful jest,
Chasing shadows like they're the best.

They tiptoe through blades, oh what a sight,
Avoiding the sneakers, quite the fright!
With giggles bubbling in the night air,
Their melody dances, quite beyond compare.

So grab a blanket, come join the spree,
Where laughter and music are wild and free.
In that grassy haven, look and see,
The joyful noise of harmony.

Serenade of the Shadows

Beneath the stars, the shadows wink,
Two jesters venture, quick as a blink.
Their serenade a playful tease,
The darkness, too, begins to sneeze.

In this symphony of chirps and croaks,
They mix up jokes, like a pair of hoax.
One says, 'Catch me!' with a hop and a skip,
But trips o'er a pebble, oh what a slip!

The fireflies flicker, giggling in light,
As echoes of laughter take off in flight.
With each silly note, the night seems to glow,
The shadows sway to the comedic flow.

So join the chorus, let worries go,
As the serenade continues to grow.
In the arms of the night, let's sing in fun,
A project of laughter for everyone!

Ephemeral Echoes in the Dark

In the shadows, loud sounds play,
They chirp and hum, oh what a sway!
Jumping 'round like they know a joke,
Wings a-fluttering, never provoke.

Bouncing high on grass with cheer,
Making music for all to hear.
With tiny feet they dance and tease,
While we laugh and try to seize.

Beneath the moon, their laughter grows,
Whispers left where the soft wind blows.
They spark our thoughts, with glee they blend,
In this night's jest, there's no end.

So let's embrace the joyful noise,
Our hearts uplifted, we're just some toys.
As day gives way to nighttime play,
We'll join the song, and laugh away!

Serene Nighttime Verses

Stars are shining, what a show,
Tiny creatures putting on glow.
Their symphony, a silly parade,
In the stillness, mischief is made.

One hops left, the other one right,
Together they squabble, what a sight!
Singing songs with nibbly delight,
As if they're actors in the night.

With every chirp, a new punchline found,
In this quiet stage, their joy abounds.
They make us chuckle with each performance,
A nocturnal dance, pure misadventure.

So grab a friend and joke along,
Join their fun, it won't be wrong.
For in these moments, laughter's the best,
As we're serenaded by their jest!

Flight of the Evening Muse

Whirling through the lush green blades,
The evening calls, funny charades.
Little jumpers take to the air,
With rhythms cool, they bring the flair.

They frolic high, up in the dark,
With every chirp, there's a spark.
A concert held, with stars above,
Their raucous tunes expand the love.

A jest, a giggle, then a turn,
In this grand show, our spirits burn.
As laughter ripples through the night,
Their antics dance in pure delight.

So when you hear that playful croon,
Join together, sing a tune.
In this spirit, together we'll fly,
With giggles and whispers as our sky!

The Language of Evening Whispers

In quiet tones, the night sketches,
A language formed with little stretches.
They chirp and click, with all their might,
A whispering joke in the fading light.

With a wink and a nudge, they'll announce,
A secret dance that makes us bounce.
Caught in rhythm, it's a playful spree,
As we join in, just you and me.

What could they mean with their silly sounds?
A punchline's waiting, laughter abounds.
Gather round and take a seat,
For the night's humor can't be beat.

So here we are, in this strange tale,
With mischief abound, we can't fail.
Let's frolic under this starry mist,
In the language of laughter, we can't resist!

Soundtrack of the Sirens

In the yard, a concert hums,
Skinny legs, they strut in drums.
Chirps and chirrups, quite the show,
Better than a TV glow.

Neighbors peek from window sills,
Wondering about these busy thrills.
As the sun dips, the fun ignites,
Dancing shadows, silly sights.

Nature's cast in insect play,
Who needs actors anyway?
With each twist, they jump and sway,
We laugh till the break of day.

So grab a snack, enjoy the scene,
Frogs join in, oh what a team!
Every song leads to the next,
Life's a jest, just like the text.

Twilight's Fabled Song

As twilight spreads its soft embrace,
Tiny critters start to race.
Under stars, they find their tune,
No need for a busy moon.

A cricket's chirp, a frog's croak,
A haunting sound, a whispered joke.
It's not mere noise but a grand affair,
Nature's laughter fills the air.

They prance and leap, it's quite absurd,
With mischief in each whispered word.
In this world, so bold, so bright,
Even shadows find delight.

So listen close, the night will speak,
In a melody, funny and sleek.
Each note is filled with starry grace,
Here's to nature's silly chase!

Syllables of the Night Air

Syllables flutter in the cool dark,
With each chirp, there's a spark.
Crickets send their ribbets wide,
   A revelry they can't hide.

Each note, a giggle in the gloom,
Like flowers that begin to bloom.
Rustling leaves join in the fun,
   A symphony for everyone.

   A little jig from fluffy tails,
  Their little voices tell wild tales.
Underneath the moon's bright gaze,
 We can't help but laugh and gaze.

So when you hear that rhythmic dance,
Just look up, you might find a chance.
To join this merry, chirpy crew,
   In this funny, raucous view!

Rhythmic Revelations

Rhythms bounce from leaf to leaf,
Filling hearts with sheer belief.
Each chirp is like a tiny bell,
In the quiet, it casts a spell.

With each leap, a joke is told,
Stories of the brave and bold.
They spread laughter from dusk to dawn,
In a world where worries are gone.

Tiny creatures, big delight,
Building dreams beneath the night.
Sharing secrets with the breeze,
Filling the air with wild tease.

So join their band, don't miss the fun,
In this theatre, we are all one.
Let loose your heart, join in the cheer,
In this midnight show, nothing's mere!

Voices Between the Leaves

In whispers soft, the night birds chat,
They gossip like old friends, imagine that.
A rustle here, a tickle there,
Making secrets dance in the cool night air.

The trees react with creaks and groans,
As the critters share their funny tones.
Their banter flows like a bubbling brook,
Not a single one reading from a book.

Each chuckle gleams like a silver moon,
A raucous laughter breaks the night's tune.
With every chirp, joy fills the space,
A riddle of sounds, a delightful chase.

Together they form a tune so spry,
Underneath the winking stars above.
It's a raucous show, no need to try,
Nature's symphony of silliness and love.

Night's Soft Symphony

A medley starts when the sun takes flight,
With gentle pings in the hush of night.
Ants in a swarm plot their parade,
As little shadows tap-dance in shade.

The moon grins wide, playing the role,
Of audience to this quirky stroll.
A froggy croak adds to the flare,
While bugs all gather, with stories to share.

The rustling leaves join in the fun,
Like instruments strumming 'til night is done.
Each sound blends well in the dark's embrace,
A curious blend in a comical space.

From light-hearted croons to playful screams,
The night brings out everyone's dreams.
In humorous harmony, they do unite,
Creating a joy that lingers all night.

An Undercurrent of Harmony

In the shadows flit a band so bright,
They orchestrate chuckles in the moonlight.
A chorus of squeaks fills the cool breeze,
A song that dances from branches to knees.

Bouncing and playing without a care,
While the rustic ground holds a quiet stare.
Who knew mischief could sound so sweet?
In this merry chaos, all creatures meet.

The night wears laughter like a new suit,
A symphony crafted from every hoot.
As fireflies flicker like jokes in the dark,
Each spark a giggle, each glow a lark.

Their nightly antics keep the spirits high,
With a wink from the stars, they dare to fly.
In this silly concert, we find delight,
As dreams sway gently in the soft moonlight.

Steps to the Rhythm of Darkness

In the depths of night, footsteps prance,
Every critter here takes a chance.
They leap and twirl in humorous glee,
Rendering the stillness blissfully free.

Chirps and flutters create a parade,
Each animal eager, perfectly made.
They skip on shadows, dance on the grass,
With a tick, a tock, as the moments pass.

Their lively tunes echo, oh so sweet,
As they tap to rhythms in the night beat.
Hilarity reigns in this grand charade,
A raucous performance, a fine escapade.

In the dark they weave laughter's bright thread,
Where silly footsteps beckon—come, tread!
A delightful jig where the playful thrive,
In this wild symphony, all come alive.

Whispers in the Twilight

In twilight's glow, the pests do play,
With tiny legs that leap away.
They chirp and hop, a lively spree,
A symphony of glee, oh me!

The neighbors frown, they hear the sound,
While dancing feet jump all around.
A rhythm strange, a comic scene,
They sing and leap, the night is keen!

The ladies laugh, they join the song,
With legs that stretch and twirls so strong.
A night of fun, with tunes so bright,
As if the world is pure delight.

Yet in the morn, they'll scurry quick,
And leave behind their nightly trick.
But still we smile, for who would dare,
Deny the charm that lingers there?

Serenade of the Night

Under the stars, they start to jive,
A tiny band, oh, what a hive!
Their clicks and clacks, a quirky beat,
That sends us spinning on our feet.

With tiny bows, they play their part,
A knack for music, straight from the heart.
The summer air is thick with cheer,
As laughter bubbles up, oh dear!

A toe-tapping tune, a sliding dance,
Revealing dreams that prance and glance.
Everyone joins, give it a try,
Beneath the moonlit painted sky!

So let them sing, these sprites of fun,
A nightly show that's never done.
With every chirp, our spirits rise,
A concert held beneath the skies.

Chirps Beneath the Moon

Beneath the moon, the mischief blooms,
With chirps and hops, they fill the room.
With tiny feet that scurry forth,
A night of laughter, joy, and mirth.

The garden's stage, they take their cue,
With silly moves, a daring crew.
They weave a tale of winks and grins,
As nature giggles, joy begins.

A chorus swell, a game of tag,
Where laughter flies, and faces brag.
No need for walls, just listen close,
When nighttime talks, the world's a boast.

As shadows fade, their whispers plead,
To stay awhile, and dance, indeed!
But when the light of dawn appears,
They vanish quick—oh, who'd have fears?

Verses on a Summer Breeze

On summer nights, the breezes tease,
With playful chirps and rustling leaves.
They twirl and leap, a frolicking show,
As laughter spreads from row to row.

Under the stars, they craft a tune,
That carries far beneath the moon.
A little jig, a hop and sway,
With every note, the world's at play.

Our cheeks are sore from laughter's hold,
As tiny dancers brave and bold.
With partners found in every spark,
They lift our hearts into the dark.

So when you hear their evening song,
Join in the fun, where you belong.
Embrace the night, let spirits roam,
For joy is found in every home.

Reverberations of Togetherness

In the night, a song so bright,
Two little critters in delight.
They chirp and twirl, they laugh and play,
Creating music in their ballet.

A rhythm found in chaos sweet,
With little wings and tiny feet.
They dance around like silly fools,
Making the night their playful jewels.

Each note a jest, each pause a grin,
In the garden where dreams begin.
They weave a tale with every sound,
A funny serenade that spins around.

So when you hear that evening cheer,
Know it's just fun, a gathering here.
With laughter echoing through the trees,
Life's little quirks, a breeze of ease.

Lyrical Landscapes

In the meadow where shadows play,
Two tiny creatures frolic away.
They jump and hop, with hearts so light,
Creating symphonies in the night.

With each chirp, a burst of cheer,
Like tickled toes, oh so dear.
They share a laugh, they share a song,
In their little world, where they belong.

Around the flowers, a painted scene,
With laughter bright, like a movie screen.
They pitch a tent of giggles near,
A banquet feast for all to hear.

So come and join this joyful spree,
Where silly sounds are wild and free.
In the realm where friendships sprout,
Life's a melody, without a doubt.

The Symphony of Heartbeats

Amidst the grass, two friends unite,
With tiny beats that feel just right.
They bounce around in playful cheer,
Creating vibrations we all can hear.

In synchronized steps, they take a chance,
Spinning in circles, a merry dance.
Their laughter rings, a joyful song,
While shadows play where they belong.

With each chirp, a giggle bursts,
In nature's orchestra, they quench their thirst.
Like little jesters, they rule the night,
With melodies that bring pure delight.

Together they craft a lighthearted tune,
Under the watchful, twinkling moon.
So let their music fill the air,
A funny rhythm, beyond compare.

Charms of the Celestial

Under the stars, a ruckus stirs,
As tiny maestros play with furs.
With each little note, a story weaves,
Of cosmic wonders beneath the leaves.

From twilight's glow, they jump and prance,
Creating a mashup, a silly dance.
Their modest stage, the garden floor,
Where giggles blend with lore galore.

In the sky so vast, they laugh and tease,
Turning void to giggles, a gentle breeze.
Each chirp a wink, each buzz a joke,
In nature's theater, where life awoke.

So tune in close, and hear their laughs,
In playful choruses of nature's staffs.
With every sound, they charm the sights,
The heavens smile at their playful nights.

Lyrics of the Natural World

In the garden, bugs start to play,
A band of chirps, in bright array.
They tickle trees with every sound,
While sleepy cats lay all around.

With tiny feet, they march in line,
Holding nightly shows that feel divine.
The moonlight catches on their wings,
As laughter from the dark world springs.

Each flick and flap, a joke retold,
In nature's choir, both brave and bold.
They don their costumes, bright and loud,
And make the silence quite the crowd.

So raise a glass to those that sing,
To every buzz and flapping wing.
Life's stage is set in evening's glow,
With laughter lighting up the show.

The Thrum of Late-night Promises

Underneath the starlit skies,
Gentle whispers, gentle lies.
A night brigade begins to rise,
With secret dreams that dance and fly.

They serenade the sleepy moon,
As nightingale hums a goofy tune.
The shadows sway, the darkness speaks,
With giggles that last for weeks.

Each chirp a trick, a playful jest,
As nature's creatures take a rest.
The air is thick with laughter's spice,
Late-night banter, oh so nice.

So join the chorus, feel the glee,
For lovers of the night are free.
In every buzz, a tale unfolds,
Of nighttime whispers yet untold.

Shadows Sing to the Stars

In the dim-lit world, shadows dance,
Playing along in a moonlit trance.
With every leap, they twist and twirl,
Silly games that make you swirl.

The starlit sky begins to sway,
Echoing the mischief at play.
While wind joins in, a playful breeze,
Chasing shadows through the trees.

They dodge and weave, they bump and crash,
The laughter grows into a splash.
With every star, a giggle's born,
As night unfolds her tales adorned.

So let your feet tap to the beat,
Of nature's concert, oh so sweet.
In the nook of dreams where shadows frolic,
Lies a world both wild and comic.

Melodies in Misty Meadows

In misty fields where giggles sprout,
A playful sound that makes you shout.
The grass is lush, the flowers bright,
    A symphony of pure delight.

With frolicking friends, they sing a tune,
    Beneath the watchful silver moon.
Each note a wink, each sound a grin,
A joyful chorus, where fun begins.

They sway like reeds in summer's breath,
    A dance of life, defying death.
The sun peeks through, the day breaks wide,
    But magic lingered, it will abride.

So come along, and join the ride,
In meadows where silliness won't subside.
Each melody a spark of glee,
In nature's laughter, we're all free.

Murmurs in the Midnight

In the stillness, whispers roam,
Little voices call it home.
Bugs in chorus, a chirpy spree,
Announcing secrets, just to me.

They joke and jive on silken wings,
Tickling thoughts that nighttime brings.
Witty tunes from grass below,
As if they're putting on a show.

With legs that dance in pure delight,
They steal the scene, quite the sight.
A symphony of wacky tunes,
Beneath the watchful, grinning moons.

So listen close, the shadows tease,
In laughter found among the leaves.
For in the dark, they play their part,
A funny song from nature's heart.

Echoing Embraces

In the night, a playful sound,
Echoes of joy all around.
Bugs in groups with tipsy glee,
Chirruping tales, just like me.

They laugh and leap with such flair,
A ticklish tune floats through the air.
Each note a giggle, a tiny cheer,
Making mischief, spreading cheer.

With every buzz, they share a jest,
In their odd world, they are the best.
Twirling shadows on the ground,
In this warmth, pure fun is found.

So raise a glass to the night's parade,
Of quirky critters, unafraid.
Their silly jests, a wild delight,
Bring smiles to all in the moonlight.

An Overture to the Quiet

In the calm, a ruckus brews,
Tiny troubadours, no one snooze.
With every chirp, they share a tale,
Of nighttime shenanigans, off the scale.

Their symphony of goofy sound,
Paints the night all around.
They tumble on, a merry crew,
While stars above seem to giggle too.

A serenade of midnight laughs,
As each little song, it crafts.
With every note, a chuckle spreads,
While nudging dreams from cozy beds.

So take a moment, pause and hear,
The silly voices drawing near.
For in their tunes, life's quirks collide,
In a night show, where joy won't hide.

Invisible Strings of Connection

In the twilight, laughter hums,
A hidden dance as nighttime comes.
Tiny kin on blades of grass,
Creating bonds that none can pass.

With every chirp, a wink and nudge,
Comedic moments, never budge.
Their subtle jive, quite a delight,
Threading joy into the night.

They play the strings of night's guitar,
Strumming tunes from near and far.
A comedic flair, a merry sight,
Bringing joy in the soft moonlight.

So when you hear their playful jest,
Join the dance, it's for the best.
For in the chorus, laugh and sing,
Life's a comedy; love the fling!

Odes to the Night Sky

In the evening's warm embrace,
A loud chirp finds its place.
It seems the band is tuning right,
For a silly concert tonight.

Hopping bugs, in joyful flight,
Dance around, what a sight!
With twinkling eyes, they play along,
In this quirky, nighttime song.

A serenade under a moon,
Hopping and chirping in full tune.
The neighbors shake their heads in glee,
What a ruckus, oh dear me!

When the dawn breaks, silence falls,
The night brigade, their final calls.
Yet memories of laughter linger,
Till the next show, they'll be a zinger!

Syllables of the Dusk

As dusk settles on grassy lanes,
The little fellows start their gains.
With silly notes they debate life,
Like comedians, there's no strife!

"Did you hear the one 'bout John?"
Each voice a pitch, they carry on.
Their chatter bounces, high and low,
A raucous giggle as they go.

Flashing wings and awkward hops,
Betting if the moon just stops.
They crack a joke at every leap,
While all the night creatures peep.

Laughter echoes in the dark,
A lively sync, a vibrant spark.
For in the night, hilarity thrives,
As silly sounds, the evening drives!

Crescendos in the Stillness

In gardens bright, they take their stance,
With each chirp, a little dance.
Whispered jokes in rhythmic tones,
A symphony of rattling bones.

Who knew the night could laugh so loud?
With chirps that tickle every crowd.
They boast of tales, both wild and bold,
In melodies that never grow old.

Audience of frogs and fireflies,
Cheering on with squishy sighs.
The insects, stars of one great show,
As goofy stories start to flow.

A snicker, a laugh, a sudden pause,
Then back to antics without cause.
In the silence, joy will bloom,
As night reveals its comic room!

Murmurs Among the Stars

Up above, the plain sky reigns,
While below, the rascals reign.
Their whispers dance on evening breeze,
Tickling hearts with perfect ease.

"Can you chirp while upside down?"
One bold critter claims renown.
The others giggle, twist and turn,
In starlit glow, there's much to learn.

With every leap and silly shout,
They share their laughs, no doubt about.
The cosmos chuckles at their glee,
What a sight, a wild spree!

From dusk till dawn, they prance and play,
Joking away the night and day.
So here's to those who sing and jest,
In the great vastness, they're truly blessed!

Night's Harmonious Accords

In the garden, under the moon,
Tiny dancers hum a tune,
With legs that jump and wings that glide,
They chirp along without a guide.

A rhyme for every little leap,
They sing so loud, they hardly sleep,
In this night of silly flight,
The air's alive, what a delight!

Two by two, they start to show,
With every chirp, a cheeky glow,
Their melodies tickle the ears,
While they giggle through the years.

As laughter mingles with the song,
The creatures party all night long,
With a chatter here and shuffle there,
Their funny world, beyond compare!

Verse of the Velvet Sky

Under twilight, on a spree,
They play and jump, just you and me,
A symphony of wiggles and pops,
With every note, their silliness hops.

Beneath the stars that start to twinkle,
They bounce and blurt, can't help but crinkle,
In a velvet sky, they leap and soar,
A nighttime show that we adore.

Swinging through the shadows wide,
They dance like peasants side by side,
With every jest, they seem to grin,
And giggles echo, let the fun begin!

Each notes' a joke, a playful tease,
They jig and jive with utmost ease,
As fleeting whispers fill the air,
In the haven of night, without a care!

The Language of the Calm

As daylight fades, the stage is set,
A silent script that we won't forget,
With every rustle and gentle quake,
The laughter echoes, make no mistake.

Their chatter dances on the breeze,
Like secrets shared beneath the trees,
With each verse, they spin a tale,
A comical plot, each detail frail.

In the hush, the giggles sneak,
With punchlines hidden, not for the meek,
Their language flows, a bubbling brook,
You can't resist, come take a look!

So listen close, their words, a thrill,
A nighttime jest that gives a chill,
In the calm, the fun unfolds,
A playful world, full of gold!

Stirrings in the Stillness

In the quiet night, a sudden sound,
Witty whispers whirl around,
The little sprites and their cheeky cheer,
Unearth the silliness we hold dear.

With each soft chirp, a giggle flows,
A chuckle sprouts where mischief grows,
In the stillness, they find their beat,
Creating laughter, oh so sweet.

On grassy mounds, they take their stand,
With springy hops, they form a band,
A funny frolic, all aglow,
They serenade us from below.

So, let's embrace their playful night,
With every chirp, there's pure delight,
As they frolic through this charm-filled scene,
In the dance of joy, where laughter's queen!

Sounds of Solitude's Embrace

In the silence of the night, they sing,
Tiny troubadours on playful wing.
Their chirps a melody in the dark,
Echoing laughter, a cheeky spark.

Shadows dance under the moon's soft glow,
Squeaky serenades put on quite a show.
With each little trill, they plot and play,
Nature's own jesters in the grand ballet.

A nocturnal choir, without a clue,
Why do they sing, just a handful or two?
In the stillness, they radiate cheer,
Tales of mischief in night's atmosphere.

Their concert a riot, no tickets are sold,
Life's little secrets they daintily hold.
As the stars twinkle high in delight,
These miniature jesters rule the night.

Nightfall's Gentle Aria

As dusk wraps the world in a silky veil,
Mischievous miniatures begin their tale.
With each cheerful chirp, they pitch a jest,
Under the twilight, they bumble and quest.

Amid the grass blades, with nary a care,
Eager to share their silly chatter fair.
An evening of laughter, you might attest,
Is best enjoyed with these tiny guests.

They dance through the fields, a whimsical spree,
More spirit than tune, oh, can't you see?
With winks and nods, they keep the show bright,
These little jokesters of the moody night.

So when you hear them, just smile and listen,
In their sweet ruckus, the heart starts to glisten.
For in the buzz and the playful spree,
Lie the secrets of laughter and harmony.

Harmonies in Hidden Corners

Nestled in shadows, a raucous embrace,
A chorus of chuckles at a curious pace.
They chirp out their tunes with a devilish glee,
In this wobbly world, the jesters run free.

Bouncing from leaf to the edge of a brook,
In the corners of night, where mischief can cook.
Their stories unfold in unspoken lines,
As they sashay through gardens, drawing sweet signs.

Tickled by laughter, the breezes comply,
Joining the fun, as the stars twinkle high.
Each note is a giggle, a wink in the air,
Echoes of joy in the midnight affair.

When the night dims low, they still won't retreat,
For pushing the limits, it's all just a treat.
This hidden ballet, what a wild sight,
As they whirl without worries into the night.

The Whispering Grove

In the whispering grove, they plot and they scheme,
Nimble and snug, they dance out a dream.
Soft melodies bubble, like laughter in air,
Frolicking freely, without any care.

A sprinkle of giggles intertwines with croons,
Bringing cheer to the stillness, beneath the moons.
Their tunes twirl around like a playful breeze,
As shadows unite in frivolous tease.

With banter so clever, they twist and they turn,
In the heart of the night, how the stars do yearn!
For these wily sprites in their glorious spree,
Play tricks on the world, oh, what fun to see!

So if you wander by, take a pause, have a laugh,
Join in their revelry, take in the craft.
For hidden in laughter, the essence we find,
Are echoes of joy, so carefree and kind.

Duet of Dusk's Glow

In the garden, sounds arise,
A symphony beneath the skies.
Bugs serenade the evening light,
With chirps and chirrups, quite a sight!

They sing of love, they sing in jest,
Each note a laugh, a playful quest.
One's high pitch makes the other squeal,
Together they dance, it's quite a deal!

With rhythm of legs, they hop and sway,
In night's embrace, they find their play.
A melody that makes us grin,
These tiny jesters, let the fun begin!

So next time you hear that twinkling call,
Just chuckle and smile, don't let it fall.
For in this chorus of silly delight,
A grand duet rings through the night!

Nature's Staccato

In the fields, the sound cascades,
A raucous laughter as laughter fades.
Tiny voices, quick and spry,
Chirping jests that never die!

With every note, a joke is shared,
A snapping twig, no one prepared.
A tap dance here, a wink over there,
Nature's humor fills the air.

They rib each other with joyful flair,
In playful battles, none do care.
With pops and zings, their stories flow,
A vibrant tune, a frolicking show!

So join the fun, don't be shy,
Let their melody lift you high.
For in this comic interlude,
Lies the heart of nature's mood!

Echoes Beneath the Stars

Beneath the stars, the night reveals,
A chorus of giggles and silly squeals.
With each chirp, a tale unfolds,
Of winks and puns, of laughter told!

In crickets' chatter, humor gleams,
A comedy club of wild dreams.
They joke about the moon's big grin,
And how the owl can't join in!

Amidst the grass, they take the stage,
With antics that show their age.
From stardust trails to shadowy dives,
These tiny jesters, they come alive!

So listen close, let laughter steer,
For night's agenda brings good cheer.
In the echoes, joy compels,
A playful night, where laughter dwells!

Ties That Bind in Twilight

As twilight wraps the world in glow,
The little live wires start their show.
Clip-clop and chirp, a daring feat,
Their stories spin with rhythmic beat!

Ties of friendship in legato lights,
They tease each other, a couple's fights.
With tiny jabs and jolly pranks,
In this grand stage, it's all give thanks!

A duet of mischief, loud and clear,
In every pulse, there's nothing to fear.
For as they chirp with quirky zest,
These bond of bugs are simply the best!

So raise a cheer to their fun parade,
In this warm night, they serenade.
For in laughter shared, our hearts unwind,
In this tapestry, we are all entwined!

Winding Paths of Whispered Words

In the garden where the shadows play,
Tiny legs hop in a humorous sway.
Chasing echoes of laughter and cheer,
Making melodies, oh so near.

Beneath the moon, the night's a stage,
Where every raspy note is all the rage.
A symphony of giggles in the air,
As if the stars are dancing with flair.

They chirp of secrets, silly and bright,
In the cloak of the dimly lit night.
With each quirky kick and jolly twirl,
Creating chaos, just watch them whirl!

So let us join this merry parade,
With silly stories continually made.
In this world of whimsy and glee,
Life's a concert, come dance with me!

Dreaming in Singing Shadows

In a world where shadows stretch and yawn,
Little voices sing from dusk till dawn.
With tiny feet twirling, quite the sight,
They create a ruckus, oh what a night!

Every rustle, a giggle, a cheer,
With jokes so funny, you cannot help but hear.
Under the gaze of a grinning moon,
Who knew the night could end so soon!

With each silly hop and playful tease,
They gather together with effortless ease.
Stirring up giggles, oh what a game,
In this raucous world, no night is the same!

So come join the fun in the shadows' embrace,
With laughter and joy setting the pace.
In this realm of merriment and dreams,
Life is a dance, or so it seems!

Tales of Tones and Touch

Hopping along on the warm summer grass,
They bring the night to life, oh what a class!
With rhythmic leaps and amusing displays,
They fill the air with whimsical plays.

Each chirp a tale, each leap a jest,
A comedy show in nature's best.
Telling stories with every resound,
In the concert of night, joy can be found!

With their tiny voices, they sing and they cheer,
Spreading laughter, far and near.
A chorus of fun, oh such delight,
Under the canvas of starry night!

So gather around, as the tales unfold,
In this lively show, be bold, be bold!
With laughter and music, heartstrings we'll tug,
In this charming dance, come join the snug!

Enigmas in the Twilight

In the fading light, where mysteries dwell,
Little figures dance; they cast their spell.
With ticklish giggles and playful prance,
Creating puzzles in their nightly dance.

What secrets are shared in whispers so low?
What funny adventures do they know?
Each leap and each bounce tells a part of the tale,
In this twilight world, they never fail.

The night is alive with riddles and fun,
As melodies twinkle like stars on the run.
With each curious sound, they'll lead you along,
In this mystery, you'll find you belong!

So unravel the enigmas, embrace the night,
With laughter and joy shining so bright.
For in every hop, there's a story to hear,
A whimsical world, oh let's hold it dear!

Ballad of the Evening Breeze

At dusk when the sun takes a bow,
A chorus begins, oh what a show!
The bugs all sing with their funny hum,
While I try to dance, but trip on my gum.

They chirp a tune, it's a wild spree,
My shoes get stuck, oh let me be!
The laughter echoes beneath the stars,
As I twirl and stumble, oh how bizarre!

Their symphony wraps the warm night air,
While neighbors peek out, with curious stare.
I wave at the moon, quite proud of my plight,
As the critters keep jiving, I join in delight.

With every note, a tickle inside,
I dance like a fool, there's no place to hide.
The breeze giggles soft, with a mischievous tease,
While I shake and shiver with joyous unease.

Shadows of the Nightingale's Tune

In shadows cast by the flickering light,
These muses croon softly, oh what a sight.
With wings that flutter, they make it a game,
While I'm just a player, without any fame.

They chirp on the fence, a cheeky refrain,
As I clumsily sway, losing all sense of sane.
With my head in the clouds, and feet on the ground,
I spin and I twirl, but I can't hear a sound.

Oh, what a ruckus, this playful brigade,
As I wobble and giggle, quite unafraid.
With rhythms so wacky, and beats so absurd,
I ask the sweet night, "Have you heard?"

And just as I think this night's all in jest,
A rat-a-tat-tat puts my skills to the test.
My laughter erupts as I leap and I twine,
In shadows of tunes, I feel truly divine.

Symphonies in the Grass

In the green underfoot, a concert unfolds,
Mischievous sounds that are daring and bold.
With each tiny chirp, a giggle takes flight,
While I'm wiggling round, oh what a sight!

They rumble and tumble, with sprightly affair,
I join in their antics, with free-spirited flair.
My dance steps get funky, I trip on my shoe,
As the critters just chuckle, oh if they only knew!

The grass shakes and shivers, the night full of cheer,
A raucous brigade speaking in ticklish sneer.
They nudge me and natter, it's all quite a jest,
While I'm spinning and laughing, I think I am blessed.

So here's to the night, and the symphonic crew,
Who twiddle and play, as I dance on cue.
Under stars all aglow, I take my bow proud,
As the grass makes me giggle, it cheers almost loud.

The Poetry of Twilight's Breath

When twilight descends with a wink and a sigh,
The air fills with laughs, and spirits fly high.
In the rhythm of night, I sway with the breeze,
While shadows tap dance, with the rustle of leaves.

The crickets are poets, with verses so spry,
They rattle my thinking, oh me oh my!
With a flip and a flop, I join their refrain,
As I tumble through laughter, it's all just a game.

In the garden, we gather, a whimsical crew,
With notes in the air, there's no time to rue.
As the stars start to giggle, I'm lost in the fun,
Who knew poetry's heart could weigh less than a ton?

So under the starlight, I revel and prance,
With each jolly chirp, I embrace the night's dance.
In the poetry spoken, with grins and some glee,
I whisper my secrets to the night's symphony.

Chorus of the Evening Sky

In twilight's glow they sing and chirp,
A melody that makes you smirk.
With tiny legs they tap along,
Creating tunes that can't be wrong.

As shadows stretch and laughter swells,
They share the limelight, ringing bells.
Each note a joke, each pause a tease,
Under the stars, they play with ease.

A duet formed in night's embrace,
With every note, they quicken the pace.
A concert that begins to rise,
As giggles hide 'neath starry skies.

So if you hear that joyful sound,
Look high and low, they're all around.
In nature's show, they're out of sight,
The evening's jesters take to flight.

Accompaniment of the Breeze

The wind comes in, a playful guest,
Whispers and giggles, what a jest!
It tickles leaves, it lifts the hair,
A dance of fun, a breath of air.

With every gust, a chuckle shared,
Amongst the trees, all unprepared.
They sway and sway, in fits of glee,
What comical antics, if we could see!

A chase begins, the branches wave,
A gentle push, they misbehave.
The breeze just laughs, "Catch me if you can!"
As creatures play in this fun-filled plan.

For in this game of hide and seek,
Every flutter is far from meek.
With whispers here and whoops out there,
The world is giggling, if you dare.

Whims of the Whispering Grass

In fields of green, they giggle loud,
The blades of grass form a rowdy crowd.
They sway and bend with every tease,
Creating laughter with such ease.

A tickle here, a whisper there,
With secrets shared, a fluffy air.
Each motion tells a funny tale,
As they invite the breeze to sail.

With shadows dancing, on a whim,
The grass grows coy, their voices brim.
They chirp and chime, in jumbled rhyme,
Making the moments feel sublime.

So join the fun, chase in delight,
Through each green patch, from day to night.
For in the rustle and the sway,
Life's humor hides, come out to play!

Nature's Secret Language

Each rustle speaks a comic phrase,
In this grand show of funny ways.
The laughter dances, wild and free,
    A symphony of comedy.

The trees conspire, the flowers giggle,
They plot and scheme, each twist and wiggle.
A wink from nature, a playful gust,
In every moment, laughter's a must.

The sun and moon exchange a grin,
While paths of joy, they both begin.
    A hidden joke in every hue,
As nature whispers secrets true.

So tune your ears, and join the jest,
In nature's arms, you'll feel the best.
For through the riddle of rustling trees,
Laughter flows like the softest breeze.

The Evening's Whistle

Beneath the stars, they leap and hop,
Their little legs, they never stop.
A chorus of chirps, a grand affair,
With silly tunes that fill the air.

They sing of love for tasty snacks,
With each high note, they twist and relax.
A symphony played on blades of grass,
Making us giggle as we pass.

They gather in gangs, all ready to play,
Jumping and hopping till break of day.
Oh what a sight, so strange yet sweet,
As the night comes alive with their upbeat.

In the cool of dusk, they start their fun,
Life's little jesters, all on the run.
With laughter and chirps, the evening's delight,
They turn the mundane into pure light.

Songbirds and Shadows

In the twilight glow, shadows sway,
As antics unfold in a breezy play.
With silly flutters, they prance around,
Their chirps echoing in the night's playground.

Feathers fluff and wings take flight,
They strut their stuff 'neath the moonlight.
With quirks and quirks, oh what a show,
Each tiny performer steals the glow.

In the garden's heart, they chirp and cheer,
Funny little dancers, no hint of fear.
Each twist and turn, a comic display,
Under the stars, they dance and sway.

Laughter entwined with the night's sweet breeze,
These jesters of joy, they aim to please.
With melody shared on a gentle breeze,
Creating a world where everyone can tease.

Dancing to the Night's Pulse

Under the moon, they begin their spree,
With tiny feet tapping, wild and free.
A jig of joy as the shadows play,
In a night filled with laughter, they dance away.

Their rhythm is quirky, a sight to behold,
With moves so funny, they're brash and bold.
The ground shakes gently with each lively leap,
As funny tales of the night, they keep.

With a blink and a bounce, they all join in,
Catching the glow where laughter begins.
From blade to blade, they spin and sway,
Telling jokes that make the night slip away.

These jolly creatures, so full of cheer,
Spread giggles and joy, year after year.
They dance with glee, they jump with zest,
Turning the night into a comedy fest.

In Tune with the Moonlight

Under bright stars, a party is set,
With all of their friends, they never fret.
Wiggling and jiggling, such a delight,
Creating a ruckus beneath the night.

They chant silly tales of ancient lore,
Adding a twist, who could ask for more?
With hops that are infectious, they surely know,
How to bring laughter wherever they go.

With each little hop, the mischief grows,
Each chirp a giggle, oh how it flows!
Gathered together, they share their glee,
In the soft moonlight, they skip so free.

So here's to the night, with its whimsical cheer,
To the dances and laughter we hold so dear.
With sprightly moves under the star's embrace,
These joyful performers bring smiles to the place.

www.ingramcontent.com/pod-product-compliance
Lightning Source LLC
Chambersburg PA
CBHW071847160426
43209CB00003B/452